PUFFIN BOOKS

# WHAT A JOKE!
## THE PUFFIN BOOK OF KIDS' JOKES

Cackles from the classroom, belly laughs from
the bike shed, giggles from the playground and
mirth from the monkey bars! Sick jokes, yucky
jokes, crazy jokes, cool jokes – more than 400
hilarious gags and riddles collected from
children all across Australia.

# What a joke!

## The Puffin Book of Kids' Jokes

Collected by
**Phillip Adams and Patrice Newell**

Illustrated by
**Terry Denton**

PUFFIN BOOKS

Puffin Books
Penguin Books Australia Ltd
487 Maroondah Highway, PO Box 257
Ringwood, Victoria, 3134, Australia
Penguin Books Ltd
Harmondsworth, Middlesex, England
Viking Penguin, A Division of Penguin Books USA Inc.
375 Hudson Street, New York, New York 10014, USA
Penguin Books Canada Limited
10 Alcorn Avenue, Toronto, Ontario, Canada, M4V 3B2
Penguin Books (N.Z.) Ltd
Cnr Rosedale and Airborne Roads, Albany, Auckland, New Zealand

First published by Penguin Books Australia, 1998

1 3 5 7 9 10 8 6 4 2

Designed by Beth McKinlay
Typeset in Gill Sans 14/19 and Sassoon 12/19 by Midland Typesetters,
Maryborough, Victoria
Made and printed in Australia by Australian Print Group, Maryborough, Victoria

National Library of Australia
Cataloguing-in-Publication data:

What a joke! : the Puffin book of Australian kids' jokes.

ISBN 0 14 038378 6.

1. Australian wit and humor - Juvenile literature.
2. Wit and humor, Juvenile. 3. Puns and punning - Juvenile literature. 4. Riddles, Juvenile.
I. Adams, Phillip, 1939- . II. Newell, Patrice, 1956- . III. Denton, Terry, 1950- .
IV. Title: Puffin book of Australian kids' jokes. V. Title: Book of Australian kids' jokes.

A828.302

This selection of jokes and riddles was first published in The Penguin Book of Schoolyard Jokes, collected by
Phillip Adams and Patrice Newell, published by Penguin Books Australia, 1997.

# CONTENTS

# Acknowledgements

Hundreds of children across Australia contributed to this collection, and special thanks go to our young technical advisers, Vidas Kubilius, Vaiva Kubilius and Rory Adams.

Teachers everywhere supported the idea for the book and asked students to write down their favourite jokes. Many thanks to Ian Burr, Michael Wright, Cathryn Ingle, Ross Deery, Heather Carter, Mark Evans and Melinda Archer. And Jean Menlove, Maria Clark and Ann Kubilius.

But the people to whom we're most indebted are the school children who found time to tell us what makes them laugh, especially those kids at Scone Public School, St Mary's, Scone, St James, Muswellbrook, Mullumbimby Adventist Primary School and Colonel Light Gardens Primary School.

# aNimal aNtics

The mummy and the baby camel were having a cuddle one day when the baby camel asked, 'Why do I have such long eyelashes?'
'Because they protect your eyes in a dust storm.'
'Why do I have such big feet?'
'So you won't sink in the sand, my dear.'
'Why have I got such a big hump on my back?'
'So you can carry a large quantity of water when you're in the desert.'
'Well, Mum, what am I doing in a zoo then?'

'I just ran into a great big bear!'

'Did you let him have both barrels?'

'Heavens no, I let him have the whole gun.'

What do you get if you cross a cocker spaniel, a poodle and a rooster?

Cockapoodledoo.

What do cats put in their soft drink?

Mice cubes.

How did the skunk phone her mother?

On her smellular phone.

What do bees do with their honey?

They cell it.

What goes wow wob?

A dog walking backwards.

**W**hat do you call a camel with three humps?

Humphrey.

**W**hat's a bear's favourite drink?

Ginger bear.

**W**hat do cats eat at parties?

Mice cream.

**W**hat do polar bears have for lunch?

Ice burgers.

**W**here do sheep do their shopping?

> At Woolies.

**W**hat petrol do snails use?

> Shell.

**W**hy do cats put mice in the freezer?

> To make micey poles.

**H**ow does a dog stop a VCR?

He presses the paws button.

**W**hat do you call a travelling flea?

An itch hiker.

`**I**t's raining cats and dogs.'

'I know, I just stepped in a poodle.'

What do you call a penguin in the desert?

Lost.

What do cats read in the morning?

Mewspapers.

`My horse is a blacksmith.'

'What do you mean?'

'Well, if I shout at him, he makes a bolt for the door.'

What does the buffalo say when he sends his son off to school each morning?

'Bison.'

How did the rodeo horse get so rich?

It had a lot of bucks.

How do you catch a squirrel?

Climb up a tree and act like a nut.

What do you call a skunk in court?

Odour in the court.

'Has your cat ever had fleas?'

'No, but it's had kittens.'

What do you get when you pour hot water down a rabbit hole?

Hot cross bunnies.

What do you call a cold puppy sitting on a rabbit?

A chilli dog on a bun.

# school daze

What did one maths book say to another maths book?

'I've got more problems than you.'

'Johnny, I hope I didn't see you looking at Mary's work then.'

'I hope you didn't too, Miss.'

`Sally, I told you to be at school by 9.15 a.m.!'
'Why, what happened?'

What's the difference between a teacher and a train?
A teacher says, 'Spit out that chewing gum!'
and a train says, 'Chew chew.'

`OK Johnny, give me a sentence with the word "indisposition" in it.'

'I always like playing centre forward because I like playing indisposition.'

How do you know if your teacher loves you?

She puts kisses by your sums.

`Sally, put "gruesome" in a sentence.'

'I was short once, then I gruesome.'

What do you call a boy with a dictionary in his pocket?

Smarty pants.

`Now class, who can tell me where you find elephants?'

'How can you lose an elephant?'

`Sally, your homework is in your father's writing.'

'I know, Miss, I borrowed his pen.'

`Now Katherine, can you spell kangaroo?'
'Cangaroo.'
'That's not the way the dictionary spells it.'
'You didn't ask me how the dictionary spells it.'

'Johnny, who was the first woman on earth?'
'Give me a clue, Miss, please?'
'Well, think of an apple.'
'Granny Smith, Miss.'

**W**hy didn't the astronaut go to space school classes?

Because it was launch time.

'Now, who can name five animals that live in the jungle?'

'One lion and ... um, um ... four elephants.'

'Daniel, if you had five dollars in one pocket and twenty dollars in the other, what would you have?'

'Somebody else's pants.'

Why was the teacher cross-eyed?

      *Because she couldn't control her pupils.*

`Johnny, you missed school yesterday didn't you?'

      *'No teacher, I didn't miss it at all!'*

`Now, what's the letter after "O" in the alphabet?'

      ' "K"?'

`Now, class, if I had fifteen chips in one hand and seventeen chips in the other, what would I have?'

      *'Greasy hands, Miss.'*

# farmyard
# fuNNiES

**W**hat do you get if you sit under a cow?

A pat on the head.

**W**hat do you get when you cross a cow with a duck?

Milk and quackers.

**W**hat do you call a duck with fangs?

Count Quackula.

**W**hat animal always goes to bed with its shoes on?

A horse.

**W**hat did Mr and Mrs Chicken call their baby?

Egg.

**W**hat kind of tie does a pig wear?

A pigsty.

**W**hat do you need to do if your chooks aren't laying?

Give them an eggs-ray.

**W**hy aren't turkeys ever invited to dinner parties?

Because they always use fowl language.

**W**hat do you call a duck that can't read?

A blind duck.

**W**hat are the knees of baby goats called?

Kidneys.

**W**hy did the farmer name his pig 'ink'?

Because it kept running out of the pen.

What goes oom oom oom?

> A cow walking backwards.

Which side of a chicken has the most feathers?

> The outside.

What do you call a shy lamb?

> Baaaashful.

What do frozen cows do?

> They give ice-cream.

What kind of horses go out at night?

Night mares.

What do you call a bull that's sleeping?

A bull dozer.

'Two of our chooks have stopped laying eggs.'

'How do you know?'

'Because I just ran over them with the tractor.'

What did the pig say when the farmer got hold of his tail?

'That's the end of me!'

One cow asked the other, 'Are you worried about this mad cow disease?'

'No, why should I be? I'm a possum.'

What do you get if a sheep studies karate?

Lamb chops.

**W**hy did the farmer light a fire next to his goat?
Because he wanted to boil his billy.

**W**hat did the duck say when she finished shopping?

'Just put it on my bill.'

What did the farmer put on the pig's sore nose?

Oinkment.

What do cows eat for breakfast?

Mooslie.

What do you get when you cross a rooster with a steer?

A cock and bull story.

Why did the cow jump over the moon?

Because the farmer had cold hands.

What's a horse's favourite TV show?

'Neighbours'.

# ghoulish
# gags

What did the monster say when introduced?

'Pleased to eat you.'

Why did the sea monster eat five ships that were carrying potatoes?

No one can eat just one potato ship.

**W**hy doesn't anyone kiss a vampire?

Because they have bat breath.

**W**hat do you call two witches who live together?

Broom mates.

**W**hat do sea monsters eat for tea?

Fish and ships.

**W**hat did Johnny ghost call his mum and dad?

His transparents.

**W**hat happened when the monster ate the electricity company?

He was in shock for a week.

**W**here do ghosts put their mail?

In the ghost office.

**W**here do vampires keep their savings?

In the blood bank.

**W**hat is a ghost's favourite dessert?

Boo-berry pie with I-scream.

**W**hat do you think the tiniest vampire in the world gets up to at night?

Your ankles.

**W**ho is the most important member of the ghosts' football team?

The ghoulie.

**W**hy do ghosts go to parties?

To have a wail of a time.

**W**hat job did the lady ghost have on the jumbo jet?

Lady ghostess.

What medicine do ghosts take when they get the flu?

Coffin drops.

Why aren't vampires welcome in blood banks?

Because they only make withdrawals.

Why did the ghost look in the mirror?

To make sure it really wasn't there.

Why do ghosts hate rain?

It dampens their spirits.

What does a monster call his parents?

Deady and Mummy.

**W**hat do you call a wizard from outer space?

A flying sorcerer.

**W**hat kind of jewels do monsters wear?

Tombstones.

What did the baby witch want for her birthday?

A haunted doll's house.

What do you call a wicked old woman who lives on the beach?

A sandwich.

Wʜat kind of dog does a ghost have?

A boo-dle.

Hᴏw does a ghost count?
One, boo, three, four, five, six, seven, hate, nine,
frighten.

'Jᴏʜnny Monster, I told you not to speak when you've got someone in your mouth.'

Wʜat do good monsters try to remember to say?
Fangs very much.

Wʜat do ghosts wear when it snows?
Boooooots.

# ridiculous riddles

What causes the death of a lot of people?

Coffin.

What word is always spelt incorrectly?

Incorrectly.

**W**hat's big, hairy and flies to New York faster than the speed of sound?

> *King Kongcorde.*

**W**hy does a steak taste better in space?

> *Because it's meteor.*

What is red and white?

Pink.

What colour is a shout?

Yell-Oh.

Why does a cat purr?

For a purr-pose.

Where do fleas go in winter?

Search me!

What did one computer say to the programmer at lunchtime?

'Can I have a byte?'

What musical instrument is found in the bathroom?

A tuba toothpaste.

How do you make seven an even number?

Take the 's' off.

What's an astronaut's favourite game?

Moonopoly.

What kind of music do you get when you drop a rock into a puddle?

Plunk rock.

What do you give a sick car?

A fuel injection.

What starts with 'P', ends with 'E' and has lots of letters in between?

A Post Office.

What do you call a fairy who never takes a bath?

Stinkerbell.

What did the teddy bear say when he was offered dessert?

> 'No thank you, I'm stuffed.'

What do you get when you cross a computer programmer with an athlete?

> A floppy diskus thrower.

What did one petrol tanker say to the other petrol tanker?

> 'What do you take me for, a fuel?'

How do angels answer the phone?

> 'Halo.'

What falls in the winter and never gets hurt?

Snow.

What did the paper clip say to the magnet?

'I find you attractive.'

What kind of dress do you have that you never wear?

Your address.

How did the piano get out of jail?

With its keys.

**W**hat do you call a scared tyrannosaurus?

A nervous rex.

**W**hy are flowers so lazy?

Because they always stay in bed.

**H**ow do you get a baby astronaut to sleep?

You rock-et.

47

**W**hat kind of bow is impossible to tie?

A rainbow.

**H**ow do you start a teddy bear race?

Ready, teddy, go!

**W**hat has a bottom at the top?

A leg.

48

**W**hy did the bank robber have a bath?

So he could make a clean getaway.

**W**hat gets wetter as it dries?

A towel.

**W**hat's an Ig?

An Eskimo's house without a toilet.

**W**hy did the hand cross the road?

Because it wanted to go to the second hand shop.

**W**hat do fairies use to clean their teeth?

Fairy floss.

**W**hy is playschool dangerous?

Because there's a bear in there.

**W**hat did the bell say when it fell into the water?

'I'm wringing wet.'

What are bugs on the moon called?

> Luna-tics.

Who gets the sack every time he goes to work?

> *The postman.*

Why do people laugh up their sleeves?

> *Because there are funny bones there.*

What is always coming, but never arrives?

> Tomorrow.

**W**hy did the chewing gum cross the road?
> Because it was stuck to the chicken's foot.

**W**hat do you put in a box to make it lighter?
> A hole.

**W**hy couldn't the sailors play cards?
> Because the captain was standing on the deck.

Wh2at did the traffic light say to the car?

> Don't look now, I'm changing.

Why did the pilot crash into the house?

> Because the landing light was on.

What does the sea say to the sand?

> Not much, it mostly waves.

What trees do hands grow on?

> Palm trees.

What room can't you ever enter?

A mushroom.

'I'd like a return ticket to the moon, please.'

'Sorry, the moon's full tonight.'

What did the piece of wood say to the electric drill?

You bore me.

Why did the sailor grab a bar of soap when his ship was sinking?

He was hoping he'd be washed ashore.

**W**here do astronauts leave their spaceships?

*At parking meteors.*

**W**hy did the lady put a sock on her head?

*Because she grew a foot.*

**W**hy is it hard to keep a secret on a cold day?
   Because you can't stop your teeth chattering.



**W**hat did the cloud say to the sun?
            'Don't move, I've got you covered.'

The more you take away the bigger I get.
What am I?

A hole.

Did you hear the story about the hospital?

No.

It's sick.

What letters in the alphabet are the best looking?

'U' and 'I'.

What can you hold without touching?

Your breath.

**W**hat did Cinderella say when her photos didn't come back?

'One day my prints will come.'

**W**hat goes up when the rain comes down?

An umbrella.

**W**hy do clocks seem so shy?

Because they always have their hands in front of their faces.

**W**hat sort of nails do you find in shoes?

Toenails.

**W**hat can you serve but not eat?

A tennis ball.

**W**hat do you call a dinosaur in high heels?

My feet are saurus.

# hEffalumps!

What did the elephant say when he sat on a box of cookies?

> 'That's the way the cookies crumble!'

Where can you buy elephants?

> At Jumbo sales.

**W**hat do you get if an elephant sits on your best friend?

A flat mate.

**W**hat do you call an elephant in a telephone booth?

Stuck.

**W**hat do you get if you cross an elephant with a loaf of bread?

A sandwich you'll never forget.

**W**hy did the runaway elephant wear green striped pyjamas?

So he wouldn't be spotted.

**W**hat do you call an elephant that never washes?

A smellyphant.

**W**hat do you give a sick elephant?

A very big paper bag.

**W**hy do elephants live in the jungle?

Because they don't fit in houses.

Why are elephants wrinkled all over?
>    Because they're too big to put on the ironing
>                                              board.

What is beautiful, grey and wears glass slippers?
>                                    A Cinderelephant.

Why didn't the elephant cross the road?
>  *Because he saw the zebra crossing.*

How do elephants talk to one another?
>  *On the elephone.*

What kind of elephant flies a jet?
>  *A jumbo.*

What do you get when you cross an elephant
with a kangaroo?
>  *Great big holes all over Australia.*

Why do elephants paint the soles of their feet yellow?

> So they can hide upside down in bowls of custard.

'Do you ever find elephants in your custard?'

> 'No.'

'So it must work.'

How do you know if there is an elephant under the bed?

> Your nose is touching the ceiling.

Why weren't the elephants allowed on the beach?

> Because they couldn't keep their trunks up.

What time is it when an elephant sits on your fence?

> Time to get a new fence.

Why did the elephant paint her nails red?

> So she could hide in the strawberry patch.

# KNOCK KNOCK

Knock knock.
Who's there?
Who.
Who, who?
What are you, an owl?


Knock knock.
Who's there?
Far out.
Far out who?
Far out man.

Knock knock.
Who's there?
Tank.
Tank who?
My pleasure.

Knock knock.
Who's there?
Turnip.
Turnip who?
Turnip for school tomorrow or you're expelled.

Knock knock.
Who's there?
Ivor.
Ivor who?
Ivor you let me in or I'll climb through the window.

**K**nock knock.
Who's there?
Sawyer.
Sawyer who?
Sawyer lights on, so I thought I'd drop by.

**K**nock knock.
Who's there?
Freeze.
Freeze who?
Freeze a jolly good fellow.

**K**nock knock.
Who's there?
Scott.
Scott who?
Scott nothing to do with you.


**K**nock knock.
Who's there?
Mary.
Mary who?
Mary Christmas.

Knock knock.
Who's there?
Olive.
Olive who?
Olive here. Who are you?


Knock knock.
Who's there?
Robin.
Robin who?
Robin you, so hand over your money.


Knock knock.
Who's there?
Roach.
Roach who?
Roach you a letter. Didn't you get it?

**K**nock knock.
Who's there?
The boy who can't reach the door bell.

**K**nock knock.
Who's there?
Fang.
Fang who?
Fang you very much.

Knock knock.
Who's there?
Lettuce.
Lettuce who?
Lettuce in. It's cold out here.


Knock knock.
Who's there?
Nanna.
Nanna who?
Nanna your business.


Knock knock.
Who's there?
Luke?
Luke who?
Luke through the keyhole and you'll see.

*K*nock knock.
Who's there?
Harley.
Harley who?
Harley ever see you any more.

*K*nock knock.
Who's there?
Boo.
Boo who?
What are you crying for?

*K*nock knock.
Who's there?
Dutch.
Dutch who?
Dutch me and I'll scream.

Knock knock.
Who's there?
Eiffel.
Eiffel who?
Eiffel down and hurt my foot.

Knock knock.
Who's there?
Justin.
Justin who?
Justin time for dinner.

**K**nock knock.
Who's there?
Nobel.
Nobel who?
Nobel, so I knocked.


**K**nock knock.
Who's there?
Minnie.
Minnie who?
Minnie people want to know.

Knock knock.
Who's there?
Troy.
Troy who?
Troy as I may, I can't reach the bell.


Knock knock.
Who's there?
Kenya.
Kenya who?
Kenya keep it quiet down there?


Knock knock.
Who's there?
Dismay.
Dismay who?
Dismay be the last knock knock joke you ever hear!

# juNglE maDNESS

'Who's the king of the jungle?' cried the lion to the zebra.

'You are, of course,' said the zebra shyly.

'Who's the king of the jungle?' asked the lion to the giraffe.

'Why, you are, dear lion,' said the giraffe.

'So who's the king of the jungle?' cried the lion to the elephant.

In an instant the elephant picked up the lion in its trunk and hurled him into the air.

'Now, now,' said the lion, 'no need to get nasty just because you don't know the answer!'

**W**hat did the snake give his girlfriend on their first date?

A goodnight hiss.

'**I**f you see a leopard, shoot him on the spot!'
'Okay, there's a leopard, now quick, which spot?'

What do you call a monkey with a banana in each ear?

> Anything, because it can't hear you.

If a snake and an undertaker were married, what would they inscribe on their towels?

> Hiss and Hearse.

Why do tigers eat raw meat?

> Because they can't cook.

Where do baby apes sleep?

> In apricots.

**W**hy did the two boa constrictors get married?
*Because they had a crush on each other.*

**W**hat kind of key doesn't unlock any door?
A monkey.

**W**hat is long and slippery and goes 'hith'?
A snake with a lisp.

Why did the lion spit out the clown?

Because he tasted funny.


What happened to the snake when it had a cold?

She adder viper nose.


How many toes does a monkey have?

Take off your shoes and count them.


What did the lion say when he saw two rabbits
on a skateboard?

Meals on wheels.

What does a snake learn when it goes to school?

Hiss-tory.

Why do gorillas live in the jungle?

Because they can't afford to live in the city.

Why does a monkey scratch itself?

Nobody else knows where it itches.

What should you do if you find a gorilla in your bed?

Find somewhere else to sleep.

How many monkeys does it take to change a light globe?
Two. One to do it, and one to scratch his bottom.

Why shouldn't you play cards in the jungle?
Because there are too many cheetahs.

# sick, sick, sick

What happened when the plastic surgeon sat too close to the fire?

He melted.

`Doctor, doctor, I'm having trouble breathing.'
'Don't worry, I'll put a stop to that.'

'Doctor, doctor, my son swallowed a bullet.'

'Don't point him at anyone.'

'Doctor, doctor, come quickly! My boy has just swallowed a pen!'

'How are you managing?'

'I'm using a pencil.'

'Doctor, doctor, everyone hates me.'
'Don't be stupid, everyone hasn't met you yet.'

'Doctor, doctor, I think I'm a billiard ball!'
'Go to the back of the queue.'

'Doctor, doctor, I'm suffering from hallucinations.'
'I'm sure you're only imagining it!'

'Doctor, doctor, can you give me anything for wind?'
'Sure, here's a kite.'

`Doctor, doctor, I think I'm a goat!'
                    'How long have you thought this?'
'Since I was a kid.'


`Doctor, doctor, I feel like a bell.'
          'Well take these, and if they don't work give
                                        me a ring.'

'Doctor, doctor, I can't sleep at night.'
'Well, lie on the edge of the bed and you'll soon
drop off.'

'Doctor, doctor, I've swallowed my camera!'
'Let's hope nothing develops.'

'Doctor, doctor, everyone keeps ignoring me!'
'Next, please.'

'Doctor, doctor, I get this really bad stabbing
pain in the eye whenever I drink a cup of coffee.'
'Try taking the spoon out.'

'Doctor, doctor, there's an invisible man in the waiting room!'

'Well, tell him I can't see him!'

'Doctor, doctor, I keep seeing green monsters with orange spots.'

'Have you seen a psychiatrist?'

'No, just green monsters with orange spots.'

Doctor?

`Doctor, doctor, I feel like a pack of cards.'
'Wait here, I'll deal with you in the morning.'


`Doctor, doctor, I feel like a curtain.'
'For heaven's sake pull yourself together.'


`Doctor, doctor, I think I'm turning into a
dustbin!'
'Don't talk such rubbish.'


`Doctor, doctor, I feel like an apple.'
'Don't worry, I don't bite.'

Did you hear the one about the boy who loved his operation?

*The doctor had him in stitches.*

'You need glasses, Miss.'
'How can you tell? You haven't examined me yet.'
'Well, I knew as soon as you walked through that window.'

A doctor had to inform a patient he had only a few minutes to live.

'Doctor, can't you do something?'
'Well, I could boil you an egg.'

`Doctor, doctor, I think I'm getting smaller!'
          'You'll just have to be a little patient.'

`Doctor, doctor, you've got to help me. I just swallowed my harmonica!'
          'Lucky you weren't playing the piano.'

'Doctor, doctor, my hands won't stop shaking.'

'Do you drink a lot?'

'No, I spill most of it.'

'Are you hurt?'

'Yeah, better call me a doctor.'

'Okay, you're a doctor.'

A young boy arrives at the doctor's crying his
heart out.
'Doctor, doctor, no matter where I touch myself
it hurts.'
'Show me where you mean,' said the doctor.
So the boy touched himself on the nose and cried
because it hurt. He touched himself on his chest
and cried because it hurt. He touched himself on
his tummy and cried because it hurt. And then he
touched himself in another twelve places and every
time it really, really hurt.
'What's wrong with me doctor?' he asked. 'How
come I hurt all over?'
'Because,' said the doctor, 'you've got a broken
finger.'


'Doctor, doctor, I feel like a dog!'

'Sit!'

# grub's up!

What's worse than finding a worm in your apple?

Half a worm.

What is a potato's favourite TV show?

'MASH'.

How do you mend a broken pizza?

With tomato paste.

What did the cannibal say when he found the hunter asleep?

'Ah, breakfast in bed.'

What kind of food do scarecrows like?

Strawberries.

What's yellow, brown and hairy?

Cheese on toast, dropped on the carpet.

Why should potatoes grow better than any other vegetable?

Because they have eyes and can see what they're doing.

**W**hy did the biscuit go to the hospital?

Because it was feeling crummy.

**W**hat's in Paris, and is really high and wobbly?

The trifle tower.

`Have you seen the salad bowl?'

'No, but I've seen the lunch box.'

What did the mayonnaise say to the refrigerator door?

'Shut the door, I'm dressing.'

What kind of apple isn't an apple?

A pineapple.

What do hungry stars do?

Chew on the Milky Way.

Where does Superman buy his groceries?

At the supermarket of course.

Should you eat your soup with your right or left hand?

Neither, you should use a spoon.

Why should you never tell secrets in a greengrocers?

Because potatoes have eyes and beans talk.

105

A peanut sat on the railway track,
His heart was all a flutter.
The five-fifteen came rushing by,
'Toot! toot!'
Peanut butter!

How do you make an artichoke?

Strangle it.

106

`Why are you dancing with that jar of honey?'
'It says "Twist to open".'

What did the tomato say to his friend who was running behind him?
'Ketch-up!'

What do you call a train full of toffee?
A chew chew train.

What stays hot in the refrigerator?
Mustard.

---

**W**hat has bread on both sides and is scared of everything?

> A chicken sandwich.

**W**hy did the steak feel suffocated?
> Because it was smothered in onions.

**W**hy did the biscuit cry?
> Because his mother had been a wafer so long.

**W**hy did the banana go to the doctor?
> Because it wasn't peeling very well.

**W**hat do you call two rows of vegetables?

A dual cabbageway.

**W**hat do Eskimos eat for breakfast?

Ice Krispies.

**W**hat stays hot in the refrigerator?

Mustard.

**W**hat do you get when you cross a hairy
monster with a dozen eggs?

A very hairy omelette.

**W**hat's white, fluffy and lives in the jungle?

A meringue-utan.

What is small, round and giggles a lot?

> A tickled onion.

What is wrapped in Glad Wrap and lives in a bell tower?

> The lunch pack of Notre Dame.

What looks like half a loaf of bread?

> The other half.

What do you call a mushroom who makes you laugh all day?

> A fun-gi to be with.

What is the strongest vegetable?

> A muscle sprout.

What did one kitchen knife say to the other kitchen knife?

> 'You're looking sharp today.'

What vegetable can draw water from a well?

> A pump-kin.

What tastes hot but always has ice in it?

> Spice.

What's a monster's favourite soup?

Scream of tomato.

What do you call a thief who only steals meat?

A hamburglar.

What nut is like a sneeze?

A cashew.

**W**hat did the astronaut see in his frying pan?

*An unidentified frying object.*

**W**hat makes the Tower of Pisa lean?

*It doesn't eat.*

**W**hat do you call a robbery in Beijing?

*A Chinese takeaway.*

Why don't bananas use sunscreen?

So they can peel more easily.

What do ghosts eat with meat?

Grave-y.

What is bad-tempered and goes with custard?

Apple grumble.

What do you get when a monster steps on a house?

Mushed rooms.

What do you get from an educated oyster?

Pearls of wisdom.

Why did the lettuce close its eyes?
Because it didn't want to see the salad dressing.

What do you call a carrot who talked back to the farmer?

A fresh vegetable.

'There is no chicken in this chicken pie.'
'Well, do you expect to find dogs in dog biscuits?'

'And how did you find your steak?'
'It wasn't hard, it was just between the potato and the peas.'

'Waiter, waiter, I'm in a hurry, will my pizza be long?'

'No, it will be round.'

117

'Waiter, waiter, do you serve crabs in this restaurant?'

'We serve anyone. Please take a seat.'

'Waiter, waiter, this apple pie is squashed!'

'You told me to step on it, sir, because you were in a hurry.'

'Waiter, waiter, there's a spider in my soup. Get me the manager!'

'He won't come, he's scared of them too.'

'Waiter, waiter, this soup tastes funny!'

'Then why aren't you laughing?'

'Waiter, waiter, how long will my sausages be?'
        'Oh, about four inches, sir.'

'Waiter, waiter, this egg is bad.'
        'Don't blame me, I only laid the table.'

'Waiter, waiter, do you have frog's legs?'
        'No, sir, I've always walked like this.'

'Waiter, waiter, what's this?'
'It's called a tomato surprise.'
'I can't see any tomatoes.'
'Yes, that's the surprise.'


'Waiter, waiter, there are holes in my cheese.'
'Just eat the cheese and leave the holes.'


'Waiter, waiter, there's a button in my soup!'
'It must have come off while the salad was
dressing.'


'Waiter, waiter, there's a twig in my soup!'
'Yes, we have branches everywhere.'

'Waiter, waiter, there's a dead fly in my soup!'
'Yes, sir, the hot water killed it.'

'Waiter, waiter, I need something to eat, and make it snappy!'
'How about a crocodile sandwich?'

'Waiter, waiter, there's a small slug on my plate!'
'Wait a minute, I'll try and get you a bigger one.'

# crazy families

'Now, little Mary, eat your greens up, or you won't grow up to be beautiful!'

'Nanna, didn't you eat your greens?'

'What are you doing there, Johnny, digging that hole?'

'I'm burying my radio. The batteries are dead.'

What do fairy children do when they get home from school?

Their gnome work.

'Johnny, it's time to get up. It's five to eight.'

'Who's winning?'

'Johnny, why aren't you playing tennis with Simon any more?'

'Mum, would you play with someone who always lies about the score?'

'Absolutely not.'

'Well, neither would Simon!'

'Polly, take that hose out of Johnny's ear!'

'But I'm trying to brainwash him.'

'Daddy, Daddy, can I have another glass of water please?'

'You've already had eight.'

'Yes, but my bedroom's on fire!'

'Johnny, I think your dog really likes me, he hasn't taken his eyes off me all night.'

'That's because you're eating off his plate.'

'**J**ohnny, I've told you not to let Rover into the house. It's full of fleas.'

'Rover, you keep out of the house, it's full of fleas.'

'**D**ad, I'm really homesick.'

'But this is your home.'

'I know, I'm sick of it.'

'Sally, you are disgusting. Why do you pick your nose?'

'Because I can, Mum.'

'Mum, I have to write an essay on the High Court.'
'Well, that's going to be difficult, paper would be much easier.'

'Johnny, you've got your shoes on the wrong feet again.'

'But they're the only feet I've got!'

'Mum, I want to learn to play the piano by ear.'
'Well, it's much easier if you use your hands.'

'Johnny, did you put the cat out?'

'Why? Was it on fire?'

'Dad, a man came to see you this afternoon.'

'Did he have a bill?'

'No. He had a nose like yours.'

Why did Johnny wear wet trousers?

Because the label said wash and wear.

'Johnny, which month has twenty-eight days?'

'They all have, Miss.'

'Johnny, that essay you wrote about your dog is exactly the same as your sister's.'

'Of course, teacher, it's the same dog.'

'Teacher, my dad said there were three kinds of people in the world, those who can count and those who can't.'

'Mum, what has a purple spotted body, ten hairy legs, and big eyes on stalks?'

'I don't know.'

'Well, one just crawled up your dress.'

'My dad can hold up a car with one hand.'

Yeah? He must be really strong.'

'No. He's a policeman.'

'Dad, are you still growing?'

'No, why do you ask?'

'Because your head is growing through your hair.'

'Dad, there's a man at the door collecting for a new swimming pool.'

'Give him a glass of water, son.'

Mum and Dad go to dinner at the local restaurant. Dad's halfway through his meal when he has a long, hard look at the potato. He calls the waitress over and says, 'This potato is bad.'

The waitress picks it up, smacks it, and puts it back on the plate.

'Now, if that potato gives you any more trouble, just let me know.'

'Look out, son! There's a ten foot snake behind you!'

'You can't fool me, Dad. Snakes don't have feet.'

'Could I get a puppy for my son?'

'No, madam, we don't swap.'

Mum and Dad were driving in the country when they realised they were desperate for a cup of tea. Finally, they arrived at a small town with a cafe. They pulled up, went inside and were just about to order when a horse walked in and sat at the table next to them. To their astonishment the horse ordered a coffee. Dad was so surprised that he asked the waitress if it was normal.

'No, he usually orders a lemonade!' she said.


'Where does your sister live?'

'Alaska.'

'Don't worry, I'll ask her myself.'


'What's small, annoying and really ugly?'

'I'm not sure, but it comes when I call out my little sister's name.'

'Mum, can I have a parrot for Christmas?'
'No, you'll have turkey like the rest of us.'

Little Johnny was six and still hadn't spoken a word. Finally, one morning at breakfast he cried out, 'Mum, the toast's burnt!' His amazed mother gave him a big kiss and hug and asked, 'Johnny, why haven't you ever spoken before?'
'Well, up until now everything was fine.'

I've got five noses, seven mouths and six ears, so what am I?

Really ugly.

'Mummy, Mummy, the kids at school say I look like a werewolf.'
'Be quiet, son, and comb your face.'

`Darling, what do you think? I just got back from the beauty parlour.'

'Too bad it was closed.'

`Mum, how can I get rid of my BO?'

'Hold your nose.'

When do you put a frog in your sister's bed?

When you can't catch a mouse.

# bush giggles

How come koalas carry their babies on their backs?

> They can't push a pram up a tree.

What did the echidna say to the cactus?

> 'Mummy!'

Where do rabbits go after they get married?

On a bunny moon.

Why do mother kangaroos hate rainy days?

Because their kids have to play inside.

What did the little bird say when it found an orange in its nest?

> 'Look at the orange mama-laid!'

What's green and smells of eucalyptus?

> Koala vomit.

Where do you take sick kangaroos?

> To the hop-ital.

What do you call a bird with a cold?

> A cocka choo.

What type of shoes do koalas wear?

Gum boots.

Why did the koala fall out of the tree?

Because it was dead.

Why do wombats dig with their claws?

Because they can't use bulldozers.

What bird can't you trust?

A lyrebird.

A young woman was out bushwalking when she came across a friendly wombat on the side of the road. She picked it up and took it to the police station.

'What should I do with this?' she asked the policeman.

'Take him to the zoo,' he replied.

The next morning the policeman saw the woman with the wombat again.

'I thought I told you to take it to the zoo?'

'I did, and this afternoon we're going to the movies.'

# totally dumb jokes

An American, a New Zealander and an Australian are sentenced to death. The American is brought out first. The firing squad takes aim. Suddenly the American yells, 'Avalanche!' In the confusion he escapes.

The New Zealander is impressed and decides to try something similar. As the squad takes aim he yells, 'Flood!' And in the confusion, he too makes his escape.

The Australian has observed this closely. He decides to follow their example. So just as the firing squad takes aim he yells, 'Fire!'

'What's that on your shoulder, Paddy?'

'A birthmark.'

'How long have you had it?'

Why was the Egyptian boy confused?

Because his daddy was a mummy.

Humpty Dumpty sat on the loo,
Humpty Dumpty did a big poo.

Why did the lobster blush?
Because the sea weed.

What did one elevator say to the other elevator?
'I think I'm coming down with something.'

`My watch needs a new band.'
'I didn't even know it could sing.'

Have you heard the joke about the garbage truck?

Better not tell you. It's a load of rubbish.

'Hey, farmer, what do you do with all the fruit around here?'

'Well, we eat what we can, and what we can't we can.'

If a steamroller ran over Batman and Robin, what would you have?

Flatman and Ribbon.

How do you confuse a gardener?
Take him to a room full of shovels and tell him to take his pick.

**W**hy did Santa Claus grow a vegetable garden?

So he could go hoe, hoe, hoe.

**L**ittle Miss Muffet,
Sat on her tuffet,
Eating her chicken and chips.
Her sister, who's hateful,
Nicked half a plateful,
And strolled away licking her lips!

147

What is Tarzan's favourite Christmas song?

'Jungle Bells'.

What's an astronaut's favourite food?

A Mars Bar.

What do you call a flying policeman?

A heli-copper.

What game do spacemen play?

Astronauts and crosses.

Why does a cowboy ride a horse?

Because they're too heavy to carry.

'Johnny,' said the dentist, 'you've got the deepest cavity I've ever seen. The deepest cavity I've ever seen.'

'Well, you don't have to repeat it.'

'I didn't, Johnny, that was an echo.'

How many magicians does it take to change a light globe?

It depends on what you want to change it into.

What did Adam say on the day before Christmas?

'It's Christmas, Eve.'